Pebble™

Polar Animals

Penguins

chinstrap penguin

by Emily Rose Townsend

Consulting Editor: Gail Saunders-Smith, Ph.D.
Consultant: Brock R. McMillan, Ph.D.
Associate Professor, Department of Biological Sciences
Minnesota State University, Mankato

Capstone
press

Mankato, Minnesota

Pebble Books are published by Capstone Press
1710 Roe Crest Drive, North Mankato, Minnesota 56003
www.capstonepress.com

062014
008214R

Library of Congress Cataloging-in-Publication Data
Townsend, Emily Rose.
 Penguins / by Emily Rose Townsend.
 p. cm.—(Polar animals)
 Includes bibliographical references and index.
 Contents: Penguins—Where penguins live—What penguins do.
 ISBN 13: 978-0-7368-2357-9 (library binding)
 ISBN 10: 0-7368-2357-3 (library binding)
 ISBN 13: 978-0-7368-9612-2 (softcover pbk.)
 ISBN 10: 0-7368-9612-0 (softcover pbk.)
 1. Penguins—Juvenile literature. [1. Penguins.] I. Title.
QL696.S473T68 2004
598.47—dc21   2003011257

Note to Parents and Teachers

The Polar Animals series supports national science standards related to life science. This book describes and illustrates penguins. The photographs support early readers in understanding the text. The repetition of words and phrases helps early readers learn new words. This book also introduces early readers to subject-specific vocabulary words, which are defined in the Glossary. Early readers may need assistance to read some words and to use the Table of Contents, Glossary, Read More, Internet Sites, and Index/Word List sections of the book.

Table of Contents

Penguins

Penguins are birds
that swim underwater.
Penguins cannot fly.

king penguins

Penguins have black
and white feathers.
Their heads are sometimes
different colors. Penguins
are many sizes.

king penguins

Penguins have fat
to keep them warm.
Young penguins have
feathers called down.

king penguins

land where penguins live

other areas where penguins live

Where Penguins Live

Penguins live south of the equator. Most penguins live near the Antarctic. They spend most of their time in cold water.

What Penguins Do

Penguins nest and raise their young in colonies.

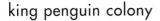

king penguin colony

Penguins eat fish, krill, and squid. They feed their young.

emperor penguins

Penguins use their wings as flippers to swim.

king penguin

Penguins can leap out of the water as they swim.

chinstrap penguin

Penguins have short legs.
Penguins waddle when
they walk on land.

king penguins

Glossary

Antarctic—the cold region near the South Pole; most penguins live near the Antarctic.

bird—a warm-blooded animal with a backbone, feathers, and wings; birds lay eggs.

colony—a group of animals that live together in the same area

down—the soft feathers of a young bird

equator—an imaginary line around the middle of Earth

krill—a tiny animal that penguins catch in the ocean and eat; krill are similar to shrimp.

squid—a sea animal with a long, soft body and 10 finger-like arms used to grasp food

waddle—to walk with short steps while moving from side to side

Read More

Hall, Margaret. *Penguins and Their Chicks.* Animal Offspring. Mankato, Minn.: Pebble Plus, 2004.

Macken, JoAnn Early. *Penguins.* Animals I See at the Zoo. Milwaukee: Weekly Reader Early Learning, 2002.

Internet Sites

FactHound offers a safe, fun way to find Internet sites related to this book. All of the sites on FactHound have been researched by our staff.

Here's how:

1. Visit *www.facthound.com*
2. Type in this special code **0736823573** for age-appropriate sites. Or enter a search word related to this book for a more general search.
3. Click on the **Fetch It** button.

FactHound will fetch the best sites for you!

Index/Word List

Word Count: 106
Early-Intervention Level: 13

Editorial Credits
Mari C. Schuh, editor; Patrick D. Dentinger, designer; Scott Thoms, photo researcher;
  Karen Risch, product planning editor

Photo Credits
Corbis, 10
Digital Vision, 8, 20
Eda Rogers, 18
Erwin and Peggy Bauer, 6
McDonald Wildlife Photography/Joe McDonald, 12
Minden Pictures/Mitsuaki Iwago, cover, 1; Tui De Roy, 4, 14, 16